The Han Dynasty: The History and Influential Empire

By Charles River Editors

A silk banner from the era

About Charles River Editors

Charles River Editors is a boutique digital publishing company, specializing in bringing history back to life with educational and engaging books on a wide range of topics. Keep up to date with our new and free offerings with this 5 second sign up on our weekly mailing list, and visit Our Kindle Author Page to see other recently published Kindle titles.

We make these books for you and always want to know our readers' opinions, so we encourage you to leave reviews and look forward to publishing new and exciting titles each week.

Introduction

Ancient illustrations from the era

The Han Dynasty

Even before the first Chinese dynasty, complex societies inhabiting the area now known as China organized into settlements, and the most important settlements were protected by rammed earth walls. The first dynasty, the Shang (1600-1050 BCE), built large walls as early as around 1,550 BCE.[1] Differing from later walls, which were built along a strategic defense line, these walls were built to enclose the settlements and areas.[2] The Shang would eventually be conquered from the west by the Zhou Dynasty (1046-256 BCE), which developed a complex system of government. In fact, it was the Zhou system's decline that Confucius (551-479 BCE) witnessed and drew from greatly for his political philosophy. The Zhou also created walled cities, and it was at this time that the first major conflicts with northern tribesman, the Xianyun, were recorded

The Zhou appear to have defended themselves and defeated the Xianyun that time, but as the centuries wore on, partially due to further attacks from the north, Zhou central authority began to break down and states under Zhou control gained increased independence. Those states then

---

[1] The Shang is the first dynasty who is historically proven to have existed. It is possible that there was an earlier dynasty, the Xia.

[2] Li Feng, ch. 3.

began to construct walls along their borders. These walls, and the walls constructed constantly during the Warring States period after the fall of the Zhou, formed an early outline for what would later become known as the Great Wall. Zhou walls were made of rammed earth or piled up stone, and some stretched hundreds of kilometers.

As the newly independent states vied for supremacy in a state of constant warfare, northern barbarians were also a constant menace. Eventually, the Chinese succeeded in eliminating many of those on their immediate northern border, but it was a bittersweet victory because it meant there was no longer a buffer between China and the even fiercer Mongols further north.[3] This new proximity led to increased cultural exchange, as well as the Chinese adoption of nomadic fighting techniques.[4]

Ultimately, it was the wall of the state of Qi that was the first to earn the name great (literally: long) wall,[5] because the state of Qin proved most adept at the new warfare and conquered all the others. It was this dynasty that unified the kingdoms under the name of China (*Zhongguo* 中国 or "Middle Kingdom"), but put simply, the Qin were a war machine. They defeated the Mongols north of the border and expanded their control there, while also fighting expansionary wars in all directions. The first Qin emperor died 11 years into his reign and was buried with the famous Terracotta warriors: These soldiers and equipment, all carved out of stone and other materials, formed an imperial army that would accompany the emperor into the afterlife.[6]

After the emperor's death, rebellion and strife took hold of the empire, and soon a new dynasty, the Han dynasty (206 BCE-220 CE), was founded. The previous emperor, Meng Tian, was forced to commit suicide, and the Han dynasty became known for maintaining a long period of wealth and prosperity during which Confucianism and other major intellectual trends in China flowered. However, they had trouble with the nomads in the north too, and after suffering decisive military defeats, the Han decided that only through a policy of peace and reconciliation could they manage relations with the Xiongnu. They offered material goods and marriages, and the border was secured, but walls were also still obviously necessary.

Ultimately, the massive investment in military expansion and conquest reaped great rewards for the Han, but all came at a very dear cost to the empire. As a result of their growing militarism, the trend of using diplomacy slowly fell out of favor around the start of the 1st century CE, but even when the old structure of peace and diplomacy with the northerners was reinstated, the Xiongnu were asked to submit to a nominally inferior position in their relationship with China. It appeared to be a compromise that would benefit both sides,[7] but soon afterward, a

---

[3] Lovell, 39.
[4] Lovell, 40.
[5] Li Feng ch. 9.
[6] Li Feng ch. 11.
[7] Lovell, 89.

Han regent usurped power and the kingdom fell into civil war. The dynasty recovered at the time, but never fully, and it continued on the path of steady decline. Local warlords gained increasing power, and northern nomads took advantage of China's disarray by pillaging whenever possible. When the most powerful and famous warlord, Cao Cao (155-220), let his control of the northern frontier slide, the Han Dynasty broke apart into three warring kingdoms.[8]

The Han Dynasty: The History and Legacy of Ancient China's Most Influential Empire examines how the Han dynasty took control of China and the impact of their reign over several centuries. Along with pictures depicting important people, places, and events, you will learn about the Han dynasty like never before.

---

[8] Lovell, 91.

The Foundation of the Western Han Dynasty

"Alas! This brat is not worthy enough to make plans with me. The Duke of Pei (Liu Bang) will definitely be the one who seizes the empire away from King Xiang (Xiang Yu). We will all become his (Liu Bang's) prisoners." – Fan Zeng

According to legend, the founder of the Han Dynasty, Liu Bang (劉邦), was merely a peasant when he was young, but despite his lack of advantages, he managed to become the first emperor of Han thanks to exceptional leadership skills. Working initially as a minor sheriff at Sishui Pavilion (泗水亭) in Pei County for the previous dynasty, the Qin Dynasty, he was appalled by the social injustice he witnessed, and thus he called upon 3,000 of his fellow peasants to rebel against the Qin government. He then took control of the Pei County and titled himself "Pei Gong" (沛公, the Duke of Pei).

A later portrait of Liu Bang

Around that time, some royal families that had been previously overthrown by the Qin government sought to restore their power, and Xiang Liang (項梁) belonged to one of them. He endorsed Xiong Xin (熊心) as the King of the Chu State (楚國). Liu Bang became Xiang's subordinate and served the Chu king, but after Xiang died, his nephew Xiang Yu (項羽) and Liu Bang were both sent by the king as anti-Qin leaders to attack Guanzhong (關中). Liu Bang competed with Xiang Yu to take the land of Guanzhong because the king promised them that whoever entered the land first would be the King of Guanzhong.

Liu eventually arrived at Xianyang (咸陽), the capital of Qin, much earlier than Xiang Yu and overthrew the reign of the Qin King, Qin Ershi (秦二世). Although the dynasty ended, the city was not in massive chaos – Liu Bang was a peasant and would not allow the innocent civilians to be killed by his army, nor would he declare himself as the king.

Xiang Yu was furious that Liu Bang gained control of Guanzhong and Xianyang before him, and Cao Wushang (曹無傷), one of Liu's men, further drove a wedge between Liu and Xiang. Xiang became wary of Liu's increasing power and influence, and most dissatisfied that Liu was going to be the King of Guanzhong. His advisor, Fan Zeng (范增), was determined to eliminate Liu because he saw him as a major threat and thus persuaded Xiang to attack Xianyang and kill Liu. However, Xiang's uncle, Xiang Bo (項伯), discovered Fan's assassination plan, and since he was a friend of Zhang Liang (張良), Liu's strategist, he warned Zhang to escape from Xianyang. Zhang was very loyal to Liu and decided to inform his master about Xiang's plan.

A Han Dynasty depiction of Fan Zeng

It was clear that Liu's army was inferior to Xiang's, and this would most certainly be a losing battle. Zhang suggested that Liu should swear loyalty to Xiang. Liu agreed, and so Xiang Bo relayed Liu's loyalty to Xiang Yu. Thus, Xiang Yu abandoned his plan and invited Liu to his banquet.

During the feast, Liu Bang sat towards the north, which signified he was Xiang's inferior. Xiang was flattered by Liu's reverence, so he patronized Liu and treated him as his subordinate. He no longer sought to assassinate Liu, in spite of the fact that Fan thrice urged him to do so. Indeed, Fan would not give up so easily, to the point that he ultimately persuaded Xiang Yu's cousin Xiang Zhuang (項莊) to perform a sword dance in the banquet hall and kill Liu when he got the chance. Fortunately, Xiang Bo blocked Xiang Zhuang every time he pointed his sword towards Liu. Liu realized that he was in mortal danger and could not stay any longer; excusing himself to go to the latrine, he left the banquet to escape from Xiang. This historical event became known as "The Feast at Hong Gate".

A Han depiction of a banquet

Liu retreated from Xianyang and killed Cao Wushang when he was back at his camp. Xiang Yu confiscated the land, set fire to the famous Qin palace, the Epang Palace (阿房宮), killed the Emperor Shang of Qin, Ziying (子嬰), and pillaged the capital. Xiang declared himself as the "Hegemon-King of Western Chu" (西楚霸王) and divided the Qin Empire into 18 feudal states.

He disregarded the king's words by dividing Guanzhong – which was rightfully Liu's – into three portions and gave each to the three surrendering Qin generals. Guanzhong was then known as "The Three Qins" (三秦).

Instead of receiving what was promised to him, Liu Bang was given the title of "The King of Han" (漢王) and a very remote Bashu region (巴蜀) as his conquest. Liu was infuriated by Xiang's decision, and he led his army to attack the three Qins in the same year, 206 BCE, and officially started the famous civil war between the Chu State and the Han State, known as the "Chu-Han contention" (楚漢之爭).

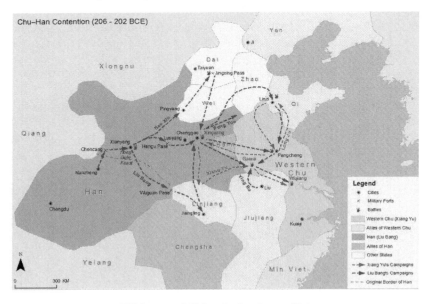

S.Y.'s map of China during the conflict

Xiang and Liu agreed to use Honggou (鴻溝), an ancient canal, as their borderline. The treaty of Hong Canal (鴻溝和議) stated that the east of the canal belonged to Xiang's Chu State, while the west belonged to Liu's Han State. Xiang retreated accordingly and released the hostages, including Liu's father and wife, but Liu violated the treaty and continued his attack anyways. Xiang lost the Battle of Yangxia (陽下之戰) and the Battle of Chenxia (陳下之戰). He further retreated to Gaixia (垓下), where the two sides fought another battle (垓下之戰).

Xiang retreated further and was about to cross the river of Wujiang (烏江) so that he could declare lordship over the small city, but he changed his mind. He said, "If Heaven wants to destroy me, why should I cross this river? I deployed my 8,000 men from Jiangdong (江東) to conquer the west, and now I live and they are gone. Even if the elders of Jiangdong still favor me as their king, how do I face and greet them without embarrassment? Even if they are silent about my lost battles, have I no shame?" (天之亡我, 我何渡為! 且籍與江東子弟八千人渡江而西, 今無一人還, 縱江東父兄憐而王我, 我何面目見之? 縱彼不言, 籍獨不愧于心乎?). Thus, he refused to cross the river and instead cut his throat.

After Xiang's death, Liu managed to take control of most of the states. As a peasant, he refused to give himself the title of emperor because he thought that it was far too noble and honorable, and a burden he could not shoulder. However, he was enthroned later, with the support of his fellow men. He preserved the name of Han for the new dynasty and established Guanzhong as the capital. His spouse, Lü Zhi, (呂雉) became the empress, and his son Liu Ying (劉盈) became the Crown Prince. He would historically be known as emperor Gaozu of Han (漢高祖).

Emperor Gaozu

Emperor Gaozu of Han knew that the empire could not be established without the contribution of his fellow liegemen, so he rewarded them accordingly, but there was an ongoing dispute over who deserved the most honor. The emperor had 18 candidates in mind, but he favored Xiao He (蕭何) more than anyone. Many disagreed with him and named Cao Shen (曹參) as the better candidate, since Cao fought and won most of the battles while Xiao was only a strategist, but the emperor nevertheless conferred the dignity of a peerage on Xiao, titled the "Marquis of Zan" (鄼侯), and Cao was put in an inferior position. Xiao later abolished the Qin law and established the country's new law.

To Emperor Gaozu's dismay, the economy and national security were not strong enough after the numerous battles with the Qin government and Xiang Yu. He wanted his kingdom to be peaceful, and the citizens to have a good quality of life, so he reduced taxes and corvée to alleviate the peasants' burden. Disbanding his armies, he offered the people who stayed in Guanzhong an exemption of taxes and corvée for 12 years, and those who left for their homeland received an exemption for 6 years, plus 1 year of full compensation. He lowered the tax on agricultural land to a rate of 1/15 of all crop yields, and reduced the amount of tribute made by the vassal kings. He also freed the slaves who had sold themselves due to poverty and famine.

Furthermore, the new ruler made a notable change to the country's ideology by putting an emphasis on Confucianism, which remains significant in the Chinese culture. Ironically, he was not a keen learner of Confucianism when he was young, and even after he had conquered the Qin kingdom, he still despised the ideology. In fact, he thought that if he could build a new dynasty with horses in battles, then he wouldn't need those theories and practices after all. A scholar, Lu Jia (陸賈), thought otherwise, and he persuaded the emperor with 12 volumes of his book, *Xinyu*

(新語), which later became a classic of Chinese literature. He asserted that Confucianism was crucial to the governance of the Han emperor, if not to the establishment of the kingdom. Emperor Gaozu was highly impressed by Lu Jia's book and eventually agreed that the Legalism of Qin was too harsh for his people, so Confucianism flourished under his reign. The emperor even prepared a memorial ceremony for the founder of the ideology, Confucius, in order to show his tribute.

A Han era depiction of Confucius

The emperor made a lot of healthy contributions to the nation, and he made clear that he was different from the emperors of Qin, but he became more skeptical as he got older. He decided to remove the title of vassal kings who did not belong to the imperial clan and confiscate their land. These people were the same group of liegemen declared as kings by the emperor himself for their contribution to the establishment of the Han Kingdom. Some were framed for treason, while others were executed. Killing a white horse, which was very precious at that time, he vowed to wipe out all the vassal kings who had no blood relation to his family.

Besides removing the vassal kings to ensure full sovereignty would remain in the hands of the Liu kings, the emperor also struggled over the matter of succession. He wanted to replace the Crown Prince, Liu Ying (Son of empress Lü), with Liu Ruyi (劉如意), the son of Concubine Qi (戚夫人)), possibly because he favored the concubine more than empress Lü Zhi and considered Liu Ying too incompetent to rule a country. The empress was desperate to secure her son's place as heir to the kingdom, so she took Zhang Liang's advice to invite the Four Haos of Mount Shang (商山四皓) to the royal court and persuaded them to support the Crown Prince. The emperor had always respected the four sages, so he agreed to keep Liu Ying as his successor.

Empress Lü was never a forgiving woman, and she remained vindictive and cold-hearted. She was furious that Concubine Qi had lured the emperor to change his heir, so after Emperor Gaozu died in 195 BCE and her son became emperor Hui (漢惠帝), she murdered Liu Ruyi with poison and turned Concubine Qi into a "Human Swine" (人彘), a person who was killed with his or her eyes blinded, limbs chopped off, tongue cut off, and ears turned deaf. Emperor Hui was disgusted by her mother's actions and took to alcohol, becoming depressed and indifferent to the affairs of his country. As a result, the empress took control of the royal court.

Although she didn't declare herself emperess, Lü held the greatest political power at the time, and while she "ruled" the country, she gradually raised the influence of the Lü family by appointing her relatives as principal officials. She enthroned Liu Gong (劉恭) and Liu Hong (劉弘) as the next emperors after Emperor Hui, known as Emperor Qianshao (前少帝) and Emperor Houshao (後少帝) of Han, respectively. Each reigned for four years but were puppet emperors controlled by the empress.

Emperor Wen and Emperor Jing

Inevitably, many despised Empress Lü for taking Liu's kingdom and gradually turning it into Lü's, but they dared not object. It was only after Empress Lü's death that they decided to wipe out the Lü clan. In 154 BCE, Lü Lu (呂祿) rebelled against the Han government so that his family could eventually claim the empire as their own, and in response, the king of the Qi State (齊王), Liu Xiang (劉襄), ordered a massacre of the Lü clan, including women and children. With the help of two loyal liegemen, Zhou Bo (周勃) and Chen Ping (陳平), Lü's campaign against the Liu family was ultimately stopped, and Liu Hong (劉恆), another son of Emperor Gaozu, became the successor. He was known as Emperor Wen of Han (漢文帝). Together with his son Liu Qi (劉啟), who later became Emperor Jing of Han (漢景帝), they created the first golden age of Chinese imperialism.

Given that the dynasty had only recently been established, Emperor Wen was prudent when establishing his system of governance. The country was weak both internally and externally at the time – they had minimal defense against rebels and foreign invasion; the citizens were poor and they had yet to build a sustainable agricultural industry to feed the nation. Emperor Wen wanted a peaceful empire, so he deployed troops along the border solely for defense purposes – he would not attack unless the nation was threatened by foreign powers. On the other hand, he focused on alleviating the burden of peasants and farmers so that his citizens could build their wealth more quickly. In addition reducing taxes and corvée, he removed some of the ruthless and cruel execution methods of Qin and also abolished a part of Qin criminal law, which stated that a criminal's family was to be punished as well. In fact, under Qin law, some family members would receive a death sentence and others became slaves.

To increase the quality of life of all citizens, Emperor Wen and Emperor Jing emphasized agriculture, and they repressed business development to decrease the control and possession of merchants and the rich. They accepted advice from their subjects with humility and modesty.

Emperor Jing

Jia Yi (賈誼), one of emperor Wen's most outspoken subjects, was the originator of this policy. To ensure the well-being of peasants and secure their rights and benefits, Jia suggested suppressing the vassal kings' power, and forbidding them to privately mint coins. His advocacy was understandably opposed by the nobility, and it was criticized by other members of the royal court since it undermined their profits. Ultimately, Jia was exiled, and he died at the age of 33.

When emperor Wen reigned over the Han Kingdom, he took advice from Chao Cuo (晁錯). Chao was just as outspoken as Jia, but he was more pragmatic in his approach to politics and its implementation. He suggested the emperor reward an honorary title to people who donated food.

This encouraged the rich people who wanted higher social status to buy crop yields in bulk; they replenished the government food storage quickly.

Chao Cuo was boycotted by the nobility as well, but he showed no fear. Instead, he asked the emperor to challenge them with courage, and Emperor Wen thus imposed heavy penalties and organized a crackdown on unlawful practices committed by rich and powerful people. He ordered an extermination of some of them, during which their blood allegedly scattered and spread through more than 10 Chinese miles. Chao's father could not stand the pressure from the upper-class society, and he told his son, "Indeed, your suggestion helps the Liu family consolidate their power, but it endangers us – the Chao family!" Chao Cuo did not listen to his father, instead remaining loyal to the royal court and doing what he believed he had to do. His father committed suicide by drinking poison.

One of the most important policies of Emperor Jing was to consolidate central power; vassal kings had excessive military power and the emperor viewed them as a threat to the Han government. Ever since he implemented Chao's policy as his top priority, he had been confiscating land from the vassal kings to cut down their resources and power, leading the vassal kings to rebel in 154 BCE, with the aim of "removing Chao Cuo the villain from the emperor" (清君側). This was known as the Revolts of the Seven Kingdoms (七國之亂), but the rebellion was settled in only three months' time.

In the end, Chao's advocacy cost him his life. Emperor Jing decided to execute him, along with his immediate family, to appease the vassal kings. Chao's father had been right, and he may have even expected this to happen when he decided to take his own life a few months earlier.

In the wake of the rebellion, the Liu family's rule over the country was consolidated and central power significantly increased. For example, the principalities controlled by the vassal kings were greatly reduced, from 46 to 26, and the regions ruled by the emperor increased from 15 during the reign of Emperor Gaozu to 44 after settling the revolt.

Emperor Gaozu had initially titled his clan members vassal kings either as a reward for their contribution to establishing the Han dynasty or providing defenses against foreign invasion. However, their power eventually grew to the extent that they dared disobey the imperial government, including the emperor's direct commands and the country's laws. To prevent another such rebellion, Emperor Jing successfully consolidated central power, increased the government's food supplies, and brought wealth and prosperity to the kingdom. This paved the way for Emperor Wu (漢武帝), whose administration focused on foreign policy against the Xiongnu (匈奴), who remained a dominant power north of the Han kingdom.

Emperor Wu

Passing his throne to Liu Che (劉徹), Emperor Jing gave the Han kingdom to his eldest son, who was merely 16 years old at the time. Emperor Wu ruled for 54 years, taking the golden age created by his father and grandfather to the next level.

An ancient depiction of Emperor Wu

The rule of Emperor Wu was the best of times for the Chinese living under the Han. It was a time when many carved themselves a place in history, including Sima Qian (司馬遷), who wrote *Record of the Grand Historian* or *Shiji* (史記). Zhang Qian (張騫) created the Silk Road connecting the East and West, and Huo Qubing (霍去病) won numerous battles against the Xiongnu as a military general. There were distinguished figures in different career fields during the reign of Emperor Wu, providing clear proof the emperor selected individuals wisely on the basis of talent.

Emperor Wu also emphasized the unification of the country and the consolidation of central power. He took advice from his court official, Zhufu Yan (主父偃), and gave permission to vassal kings to share their principalities within their kinship network. The purpose of this policy was clear, since dividing the land into smaller portions diluted the power of the vassal kings. Emperor Wu was wise to implement this measure, and during his reign the imperial government didn't even deem it necessary to deploy military troops because the vassal kings became steadily more powerless over time and were no longer a threat to the royal family. Furthermore, the emperor restricted contact between merchants, vassal kings, and nobility to prevent collusion, and they were not allowed to participate in the royal court. The threat imposed by vassal kings had finally been eliminated after three generations of imperial rule.

Having solved the deep-rooted conflict between the imperial family and the vassal kings, the emperor reformed the royal court as well. After the establishment of the Han dynasty, Emperor Gaozu made Xiao He and Cao Shen chancellors, a position that obeyed only the emperor. Initially serving as the right-hand man of the emperor, Chancellors eventually held massive political power over time, until they were so powerful that Emperor Jing could not make decisions as he pleased without asking his chancellor, Zhou Yafu (周亞夫) first.

When Liu Che was enthroned as the emperor, Tian Fen (田蚡) was appointed as his chancellor. He promoted a civilian to an official of exalted rank, while skipping all the necessary official procedures. Even worse, he dared to request using government land to build his own mansion. Emperor Wu was indignant, and sarcastically asked him, "Why don't you use our military base instead?" The emperor tried to reduce the power of the chancellor by constantly changing the people who held the position. 13 were appointed and dismissed during the 54 years of his reign, and their fates weren't pleasant. Three were executed, another three were sent away, two committed suicide, and another three died shortly after being removed. He also transferred some of the chancellor's duties to two generals, Wei Qing (衛青) and Huo Qubing, and his other subjects.

Continuing the tradition put in place by his predecessors, Emperor Wu showed respect to Confucianism, but only on the outside, as he privately favoured Legalism. Legalism usually disregarded morality and focused on consolidating the power of the central government by implementing a series of laws that escalated fines and punishments. This Chinese philosophy was especially powerful when it came to preventing revolts and increasing the government's reserves, which were essential for the long battles with the Xiongnu. Emperor Wu believed that the first step to conquering a foreign power was neither training the army nor employing military strategies, but rather taking complete control of his own kingdom. Thus, he amended the law to the extent that it nearly matched the cruelty of Qin's law, and he undid the efforts of his predecessors to abolish the Qin laws. For example, those who did not report a crime they witnessed were just as condemnable as the criminal, and a lot of people were executed as a result of this law.

Initiating a series of wars on the borderline, especially towards the Xiongnu in the north of the kingdom, the emperor colonized the surrounding land and made China far superior than its foreign counterparts. Since the end of the Qin dynasty, Chinese peasants were constantly troubled by the Xiongnu, who were so fierce that they had even attacked areas near the capital, Chang An (長安). The issue was one that worried Emperor Wu a lot, enough to compel him to put it at the top of his list. He was so determined in the matter that he commanded some highly competent generals such as Li Guang (李廣), Wei Qing (衛青), and Huo Qubing (霍去病) to conquer the northern land. They destroyed the numerous forces of the Xiongnu and continued marching towards the north. The Han kingdom incorporated a few more states, and the emperor ordered his people to migrate to those areas. These extra states bridged the gap between the Han kingdom and countries in the West and helped connect the Silk Road, which furthered Chinese influence and trade with foreign countries.

To further increase the monetary reserve for military purposes, Emperor Wu also adopted some new policies and boosted the national economy. First, he established a system of 11 honorary titles (武功爵) as an incentive for rich people who would pay to become government officials and upgrade their social status. Second, the central government issued a unified currency for the whole nation and made the materials and the minting procedures of the coins exclusive to the government. This stopped the vassal kings from minting coins for their own state as they previously did, and effectively prevented the nobility from privately and illegally minting coins as well. Third, Emperor Wu made the salt industry and iron industry government-owned, controlling the supply and unifying the price of the two essential resources. The revenue was used to pay off military expenses and the luxurious spending of the royal family. Fourth, he adopted market control for certain products, and by using the buy low-sell high strategy, he significantly increased the government's revenue.

Although his reign might seem to have led the Han kingdom to prosper, it also brought the development of the Western Han Dynasty to its peak, and by the end, the emperor had used almost all the reserves for the military and his luxuries. After his reign, the country was no longer superior to the Xiongnu, marking the beginning of the Liu family's downfall.

Emperor Zhao and Emperor Xuan

According to Han tradition, the eldest son succeeded his father, but this was not the case for Emperor Wu. In his later years, he favored Consort Zhao, who was titled as Lady Guoyi (鈎弋夫人), more than Empress Wei Zifu (衛子夫). The Crown Prince, Liu Ju (劉據), was born to the empress, while Prince Fuling (弗陵) was born to Consort Zhao. There were rumors that Prince Fuling would replace the Crown Prince and become the king, though Emperor Wu never shared his thoughts on the matter. However, one of the emperor's subjects, Jiang Chong (江充), framed the Crown Prince, implicating him in witchcraft practice against the emperor and forcing Liu Ju to defend himself with his own troops against the royal army. Defeated by the imperial military and convicted of treason, Liu Ju was exiled as a result. He and his mother committed suicide later, feeling bitter and betrayed.

Emperor Wu was guilt-ridden after finding out the truth, and though he executed Jiang Chong and his relatives, he knew that could never bring his son back. He needed to move on and pick a new successor who would be able to maintain the prosperity of his kingdom. He was already 62 when Prince Fuling was born, and he knew that he wouldn't live long, but while Prince Fuling was the best candidate, he was too young. As a result, Emperor Wu appointed Huo Guang (霍光) as regent to assist Liu Fuling, later known as Emperor Zhao (漢昭帝), who was merely 8 years old when he was put on the throne. In fear that Consort Zhao might become the next Empress Lü, Emperor Wu killed his beloved spouse shortly before he died.

Emperor Zhao

A portrait of Huo Guang

With Huo as the main regent and Jin Midi (金日磾), Shangguan Jie (上官桀) and Sang Hongyang (桑弘羊) as co-regents, Emperor Zhao adopted policies to help replenish the government's monetary reserves and maintain peace for the kingdom. Since he was young at the time of his ascension, Huo made the major decisions and controlled the royal court while the emperor's older sister, Princess Eyi (鄂邑公主), took care of the palace. Everything seemed to be going smoothly, but a group of people were planning a revolt. The vassal king of the Yan State (燕國), Liu Dan (劉旦), was appalled by the ascension of Emperor Zhao because, as Emperor Wu's second son, he believed he should have become Crown Prince upon his brother's death. He collaborated with Liu Zhang (劉長) and Liu Ze (劉澤) from the imperial clan and planned to overthrow Emperor Zhao by accusing him of being an illegitimate child of Emperor Wu. The plan was ultimately revealed, leading Huo Guang to execute Liu Zhang and Liu Ze, but Liu Dan was not punished because he was the son of the deceased Emperor Wu.

Undeterred, Liu Dan remained remorseless and planned another revolt, this time with the objective of removing Huo Guang from his well-established position to help his associate, Shangguan Jie the co-regent, get more power over Huo Guang. Interestingly, Huo and Shangguan were initially friends, and Huo's daughter and Shangguan's son, Shangguan An (上官安), were even married with a 5 year old daughter around the time of the rebellion. Shangguan Jie wanted his granddaughter - even at such a young age - to become the empress of Emperor Zhao, in the hope of getting more power in the royal court, but his suggestion was denied by Huo.

Once that plan failed, he urged his son to turn to Ding Wairen (丁外人), who was the lover of Princess Eyi. Princess Eyi later agreed to help them, in exchange for their assistance in making Ding the prince consort. The 5-year-old girl soon became the empress, and the revolt intended to kill Huo at a banquet, but the rebellion was once again unsuccessful: Huo later executed Shanggaun Jie, Shangguan An, Sang Hongyang and Ding Wairen, but he spared his granddaughter, Empress Shangguan, due to her young age. Liu Dan committed suicide after these two failures, and Princess Eyi killed herself after the death of her lover. Huo became the only regent left (Jin Midi was dead by this time), and his power further increased. Emperor Zhao continued to rely on him afterwards.

Emperor Zhao died of disease at the age of 22, and Huo believed that the Prince of Guangling (廣陵王), Liu Xu (劉胥), was not capable of ruling a country. Thus, he installed Emperor Zhao's nephew, Liu He (劉賀), who was known as the Marquis of Haihun (海昏侯), as the successor. Huo deposed him after 27 days because the new king often went against him and then appointed the grandson of Liu Ju, Liu Xun (劉詢), as the next emperor. Liu Xun became known as Emperor Xuan (漢宣帝).

A portrait of Emperor Xuan

Emperor Xuan was a commoner who was born outside the palace due to his father's unjust punishment for practicing witchcraft and was therefore never connected with any royal court officials. In other words, Huo Guang would have easily controlled him. However, growing up as an ordinary person, he understood the suffering and difficulties faced by his people, so his policies tended to be lenient towards citizens. Emperor Xuan was young at the time, but not naïve, and he knew that Huo Guang was the most powerful person in the royal court, even stronger than he was. Emperor Xuan was relatively humble and polite to Huo before Huo died of old age, but there was quite a conflict between them on the matter of choosing an empress. Huo Guang's wife wanted to make her daughter the empress so that the emperor would be further controlled by the Huo family, and plenty of the imperial officers supported Huo's suggestion, but the emperor favored Lady Xu (許氏), and he wanted her to become his empress.

Angered and dissatisfied by the emperor's decision, Huo Guang's wife poisoned Lady Xu when she was giving birth to a child, and once Lady Xu was dead, Huo Guang persuaded the emperor to take his daughter as empress. The child became the Crown Prince a year later. Although Huo's wife told the empress to poison the Crown Prince just as she had Lady Xu, they were unsuccessful this time.

In 68 BCE, Huo Guang died of disease, and Emperor Xuan began to gain more power over the Huo family despite the fact the Huo clan members were still in dominant positions in different fields of the government. To counteract this, the emperor slowly transferred their powers to other loyal subjects. For example, he titled the Crown Prince's grandfather, Xu Guanghan (許廣漢), and his brothers as marquis, and he lowered the officer ranking of the Huos. The Huo family was naturally indignant, in part because they had contributed so much to the Han government by assisting the previous emperors. The family planned a revolt against the government, but the conspiracy was discovered, and the Huos were either executed or committed suicide. Empress Huo was renounced, and families connected with the Huos were punished.

In all, Emperor Zhao and Emperor Xuan promoted wealth and prosperity. They both agreed to establish Huo's administrative policies for the country, such as reducing taxes and corvée, and these policies compensated for the luxurious and military spending of Emperor Wu, bringing the country to another era of peace before the empire's decline.

The End of Western Han Dynasty

In 49 BCE, Liu Shi (劉奭), the eldest son of Emperor Xuan, ascended to the throne and became known as Emperor Yuan of Han (漢元帝). Emperor Yuan was kind and gentle, and though he might not have been the best ruler, he had a good heart. His well-mannered personality was a double-edged sword that offered strengths and weaknesses. For example, when Liu Shi was still a Crown Prince, he favored Consort Sima (司馬良娣) so much that he became depressed after she died of disease. It was very rare for a Crown Prince to mourn and grieve for a woman when he could have as many replacements as he wanted, but he was a young man who fell in love and didn't know much about ruling a country. Put simply, he was idealistic and naive.

Having learned mostly about classic Confucianism, he largely supported the philosophy and despised his father for adopting Legalism to rule the kingdom. He was disgusted by all those punishments on the people, and he had an ideal in his mind that everyone would obey the teachings of Confucius and be civil to others.

Emperor Xuan once said that his son would bring the downfall of the Han kingdom, and he would prove prescient. In fact, Emperor Xuan even wanted to change the Crown Prince, but remembering that Liu Shi was born to Empress Xu, the woman he married when he was merely a commoner, he decided to give his son a chance.

Before Emperor Xuan died, he appointed Shi Gao (史高), Xiao Wangzhi (蕭望之), Zhou Kan (周堪) as regents. Xiao was supportive of Confucianism, therefore, Emperor Yuan valued his suggestions and used mostly the policies he proposed to rule the country. They made Confucianism the national ideology, but Shi disagreed. Shi thought that the use of Legalism – or at least using Confucianism on the outside but using Legalism on the inside – was best for ruling the country, just as Emperor Xuan had agreed on previously.

Soon, Xiao gained more power than Shi in the royal court, the opposite of when Emperor Xuan reigned. Shi was angered by the tide turned; together with the eunuchs, they refuted all of Xiao's proposals to the king. Xiao once persuaded the Emperor to take the eunuchs off a position called Zhong Shu (中書), which was responsible to relate the Emperor's messages to other officers. Xiao believed that the eunuchs neither deserved the post, nor were they qualified, since they were castrated. Emperor Yuan, indecisive and hesitant as always, did not do so. The eunuchs remained powerful in the court, but they felt insulted by Xiao. Later, some eunuchs such as Hong Gong (弘恭) and Shi Xian (石顯) allied themselves to Shi Gao; they had the same objective of removing Xiao from the court. They told the Emperor that Xiao merely wanted to get all the powers by refuting the suggestions they made, and they got Xiao arrested.

Xiao thought that it was meaningless if the Emperor didn't trust him; he was already in his 60s, and he was not about to spend the rest of his life in prison, so he committed suicide by drinking poison. Emperor Yuan was shocked after hearing the news of Xiao's death. He grieved for Xiao, and berated Hong Gong and Shi Xian for tormenting his regent. However, he did no more to punish them. He was the forgiving king who didn't know how to avenge his losses.

Gradually, there was a contention between the Shi family, the eunuchs and the Confucians. After Xiao died, Hong died of disease that same year. Shi Xian took the job position of Zhong Shu, and slowly he gained more power than all other parties. Emperor Yuan was too naive: he thought that the eunuchs would be faithful because they could not build a family and so they would not end up being as powerful as the Shi family. He trusted Shi Xian too easily, especially in his later years, when he was sick, so that Shi come to hold even greater political power over the Emperor. Every imperial official knew that Shi was the one who made the decisions. Shi Xian (石顯) allied himself to the Shi (史家) and Xu family (許家), as well as some of the Confucians; he eventually built a powerful network in the royal court.

When the next king Liu Ao (劉驁), known as the Emperor Cheng (漢成帝), ascended to the throne, he was left with the problem of overly powerful eunuchs, but he made thing worse over time. Emperor Yuan knew that his son focused more on self-indulgences than on the matters of the kingdom. He wanted to change the Crown Prince but he was very indecisive: when Shi Dan (史丹) cried for Liu Ao and begged the Emperor to change his mind, Emperor Yuan was touched by him. He told Shi to take care of his son and the kingdom after he died. After Liu Ao was put on the throne, his mother Wang Zhengjun (王政君) gained more power for her family in the royal court, but this did not happen without the support from Emperor Cheng himself.

Having the greatest power in the royal court, Shi Xian was the first to be boycotted by Emperor. To do that, Emperor Cheng built a good relationship with other royal families who were not of the Liu imperial clan. They reported to the kings some of the Shi's past wrongdoings, so that the Emperor could have an excuse to dismiss the eunuch. However, those royal families turned out to gain more power in doing so. On the other hand, Emperor Cheng collaborated with the Wang family to boycott other royal families such as the Feng family (馮家) and the Xu family (許家). As a result, the older brother of empress Wang, Wang Feng (王鳳), became the winner of the game. Many of the Wang clan became marquis, including Wang Mang (王莽), who later ended the Western Han dynasty.

When Emperor Cheng died of stroke, he did not have a son to be his successor. His nephew, Liu Xin (劉欣), ascended to the throne instead. He was Emperor Ai of Han (漢哀帝). Most scholars suspected that Emperor Ai was homosexual, since he had a very deep relationship with Dong Xian (董賢). The idiomatic term for homosexuality in ancient Chinese, "The passion of cut sleeve" (斷袖之癖), was created out of their story. When Emperor Ai died, he wanted to give his throne to Dong Xian, but grand empress Wang ignored his last wish; instead, she appointed Wang Mang as regent to help the next king, Liu Kan (劉衎), the cousin of Emperor Ai, because the Emperor died childless. Dong committed suicide shortly after Emperor Ai died.   Liu Kan was known as Emperor Ping of Han; he was merely nine at the time of his ascension to the throne. As a result, Wang Mang easily seized power in the royal court. He died after seven years of reign. Some said that he died because of heart disease, other said that Wang Mang poisoned the king so that he could choose another puppet monarch.

Wang wanted to be the Emperor himself, but he thought that it was not yet the time for him to declare himself a king. Therefore, he chose the youngest among all potential successors, Liu Ying (劉嬰), as titular head of the kingdom. However, Liu Ying was not officially an Emperor; he was still a prince who was controlled by Wang. People called him Ruzi (孺子) instead of treating him formally as an Emperor. Wang even forbade other people to communicate with him and he isolated him from the outside world. As a result, Liu could not speak well and had only minimal knowledge about the world as he grew up. With a young and uneducated puppet, Wang was on the right path to build his own dynasty.

Xin Dynasty of Wang Mang

The imperial Liu clan members knew that Wang Mang was stealing their power; he was merely a hypocritical person who could never be trusted. Besides, a lot of officers left the royal court because they refused to swear loyalty to Wang. The kingdom continued to weaken without talented statesmen. Angered by Wang's dictatorship, Liu Chong (劉崇) led his army against Wang. He failed and died in the war. A royal official, Zhai Yi (翟義), rebelled against Wang as well. He installed Liu Xin (劉信), a marquis from the Liu clan, as the new Emperor. Since the ancient Chinese thought that the Emperor was the son of god, most despised Wang for making himself the Emperor because his act went against the will of god.

Some vassal kings agreed with Zhai that the empire should be run by the Liu family. They joined the revolt to reinstall the power of Liu. Wang controlled the royal troops and he was too powerful to be defeated; Zhai and others failed as well. Later, the peasants formed their own army against Wang because they also thought that he broke the command of god. They planned to have Liu Xuan (劉玄), Liu Penzi (劉盆子), or other Liu family members ascend to the throne. Wang was worried about the large-scale army – he promised that he would retire after Ruzi grew up. However, once the rebellion army was defeated, he only became prouder and more ambitious. He thought that if he could settle all those revolts, then god must have wanted him to become the true Emperor. He needed to prove this to his people however. When Ai Zhang (哀章) wrote a false prophecy claiming that it was god's will that Wang ascend to the throne, Wang declared himself the new Emperor, on the premise of fulfilling the will of god. He called his dynasty the Xin dynasty (新朝) – its literal meaning being "the new dynasty" – and officially ended the Western Han period.

Since the national power had declined a lot at the end of the Western Han, Wang adopted policies which aimed at bringing back peace to society. He was a Confucian and so he used this ideology to rule the country. He confiscated all the private land and turned it into government-owned land; he forbade the people to sell any land or slave; he changed the currency and the officer titles. Salt, iron and alcohol also became government-owned property. People voiced an objection to those policies, but Wang legislated them anyways and imposed heavy punishments on people who violated the new law. Wang did not bring peace to the nation with those impractical policies however. He only worsened the situation – a lot of commoners were arrested by the new law. Wang then changed the law frequently that it became hard to implement it; he created more chaos than the people could bear.

Wang was also terrible at his diplomacy. He forced the Qiang people (羌人) to give up their coastal state so that Wang could get an additional state on top of the three coastal states he already ruled. He called them "Si Hai" (四海), meaning "The Four Seas", which in the ancient times signified that Wang's collection was complete because each sea was located in one of the four directions. He forced people to migrate to the new state, to the extent that he created fifty more laws to frame people with all sorts of crimes and exile them to the state. On the other hand, he downgraded the king of Xiongnu (匈奴), Goguryeo (高句麗) (ancient Korea), and some other western countries – who previously submitted to Han as tributary kings – to marquis. He challenged foreign powers without a second thought, even when his kingdom itself was falling apart. This caused a lot of border conflicts, and national defense grew weaker as well.

Wang only cared about himself and his family; he hired about 300 people from his own clan to be the government officials to replace the Lius and the people who left. While he had a luxurious life as an Emperor, his people could only eat tree barks to survives while commodity prices soared. Furthermore, the monetary reserve was emptied because of the natural disasters around the kingdom. Revolts took place everywhere and everyday since more people had started to realize that their king was too selfish to improve their quality of life. One very interesting revolt – the first female revolt leader – was Lü Mu (呂母). Her son was executed according to the biased laws legislated by Wang. To take revenge for her beloved son, she killed the state officer, but she died of disease before she could overthrow Wang. Soon, two biggest rebellion armies were formed: the Green Forest (綠林軍) from the south and the Red Eyebrows (赤眉軍) from the north.

The Green Forest was first to enter the capital, Chang An (長安). Wang had his officer Wang Yi (王邑) guard the palace while he escaped to Jian Tai (漸台) with a thousand of his subjects. Wang Yi's son and some other officials who stayed in the royal court were about to escape, but Wang Yi insisted that they should guard the palace till their last breath. Meanwhile, Wang Mang's followers were all killed by the Green Forest; he himself was killed by a merchant named Du Wu (杜吳). The Green Forest cut off Wang's head and hung it by the city gate. Later, his head became an item in the collection of the royal families, until the Jin Dynasty (晉朝) in 295 BCE. The Xin dynasty had only lasted 14 years before it ended.

The Founding of the Eastern Han Dynasty

The Green Forest installed Liu Xuan; he was known as the Gengshi Emperor (更始帝). However, the Red Eyebrow installed Liu Penzi instead. Another party even claimed that Ruzi Ying was the real son of god because he had the purest royal bloodline. Liu Xuan ordered Li Song (李松) to attack Ruzi's campaign; Ruzi died when he was only 21 after being controlled by all sorts of people in his tragic life. Nevertheless, the contention between the Green Forest and the Red Eyebrow continued. Liu Xiu (劉秀) saw the opportunity to become the Emperor out of the chaos caused by the two rebellion armies. He was Emperor Guangwu (漢光武帝), who successfully pieced the divided kingdom back together and brought prosperity into the Han empire again.

Emperor Guangwu had an exceptionally good heart; he thought that ethics and morals were what made humans human. This was one of his best leadership skills, which made people respect and admire him. When he was fighting with the Red Eyebrow, one of his subjects suggested that the king should make the canal embankment of the Yellow River collapse to drown their opponents, but the king refused to do so even if it meant an easy victory. The Emperor even forgave the murderer of his own brother, the Gengshi Emperor. He made him a marquis when Liu Xuan fled for his life. Even so, Liu Xuan was killed by the Red Eyebrow later and Emperor Guangwu grieved for his loss.

Keeping his people in mind, Emperor Guangwu adopted a series of policies to improve the economy and to increase the population. He reduced taxes and corvée, and released slaves and criminals as well. One serious problem consisted of rich landowners who had obtained their lands illegally. The Emperor ran a program similar to the census, called the Du Tian system (度田制度) to count the population and measure the land they owned accordingly. This helped set up restrictions for landowners and established another source of government income from the rental property tax. The Emperor even executed the convicted landowners to show his determination in correcting the bad practice.

The policies of Emperor Guangwu increased national power and built a positive diplomatic relationship with foreign countries. This was followed by an era of peace for the Han kingdom, under the rule of Emperor Ming and Zhang.

The Rule of Emperor Ming and Zhang

After Emperor Guangwu died, Liu Zhuang (劉莊) became his successor even though he was the fourth son. He was Emperor Guangwu's favorite son because he had shown his potential since he was a kid – he could read difficult Chinese classics on Confucianism such as the *Spring and Autumn Annals* (春秋) and the *Book of Documents* (尚書). He was known as Emperor Ming (漢明帝); he basically adopted Emperor Guangwu's policies and promoted the agriculture industry. In 75 AD, the Emperor died and the Crown Prince Liu Da (劉炟) ascended to the throne. He was Emperor Zhang (漢章帝), and together with his father, their governance was comparable to that of Emperor Wen and Jing during the Western Han dynasty.

Emperor Ming and Zhang both had a mission to maintain the prosperity of the kingdom. They learned from the story of Wang Mang – who was from a royal family but not of the Liu clan – that nobility was not to be trusted. Therefore, they imposed heavy punishments on their officials, especially to the powerful royal families, even if they only committed small crimes. Emperor Ming's younger brother, Liu Ying (劉英) even committed suicide for his crime; a lot were executed regardless of the level of their positions. Other than that, he was very patient with his officers, and he paid attention to their proposals without partiality. Emperor Zhang was more lenient than his father however. He lessened the punishment for corruption. According to the law established by previous Emperors of Eastern Han, corrupted officers and their next three generations were forbidden to become the royal officials, but the Emperor abolished this law.

When there was a drought in several states, people believed that god was punishing them for creating such harsh laws that caused innocent people to be arrested and executed. The Emperor believed this as well, and released the prisoners. The Emperor wasn't necessarily benevolent, but it was true that he implemented some virtuous policies because he was superstitious.

The two Emperors supported mostly Confucianism, and it was during their times that Buddhism became more prevalent in the country. Emperor Ming first sent Cai Yin (蔡愔) and Qin Jing (秦景) to ancient India to obtain some Buddhist texts, and he built the first Buddhist temple in Chinese territory, the White Horse Temple (白馬寺). On the other hand, ever since the end of the Western Han, there were records of flood in states along the river. Emperor Ming ordered the construction of canal embankments along the Yellow River. The construction effectively avoided death and casualty from the natural disaster.

Both Emperor Ming and Zhang took a more aggressive approach towards the Xiongnu than Emperor Guangwu had. During the end of the Western Han and the Xin dynasty, there were frequent border conflicts initiated by the Xiongnu. At the time of Emperor Ming, the Xiongnu was divided into the north Xiongnu and the south Xiongnu. The south Xiongnu gradually integrated themselves to the Han country, but the north Xiongnu often attacked the empire. Emperor Ming sent Ban Chao (班超), a very famous diplomat and general, to other Western countries and persuaded them to disconnect with the Xiongnu in exchange of a good relationship with the Han kingdom. With only 36 people, he beat hundreds of Xiongnu with his exceptional leadership skills. Emperor Zhang also sent Dou Xian (竇憲) to attack the north Xiongnu, and they won the battle as well.

The time of Emperor Ming and Zhang could be considered as the best period of the Eastern Han era. However, Emperor Zhang was rather lenient towards the nobility and the eunuchs. For example, Dou Xian was the brother of Empress Dou, but he allowed him to be one of the top royal officers despite his background. The contention between nobility and the eunuchs would become the major cause for the end of the Eastern Han dynasty.

The Rule of Other Eastern Han Emperors

In 88 AD, Emperor Zhang died and his fourth son Liu Zhao (劉肇) ascended to the throne; he was Emperor He (漢和帝). He was born to Consort Liang (梁貴人) but she died depressed after Empress Dou made false accusations against her. Empress Dou thus became the stepmother of Emperor He, but she took care of him well, as if he was her own son. Liu Zhao was only 9 years old when he took the throne, so Empress Dou became responsible for making decisions in the royal court. She promoted her elder brother, Dou Xian, and her younger brothers.

The Dou family, thus, held enough power to run the government. Empress Dou became the dictator who seldom listened to officers' proposals. The officials persuaded the empress to attack the Xiongnu; they even berated her for giving up the lives of thousands of people and failing to eliminate the threat of the Xiongnu on the border. Even so, she didn't change her mind and decided everything as she pleased. The Dou family was the sole player of the game; Dou Xian even trained his own assassinators to kill people he disliked. When Emperor Ming reigned over the kingdom, Dou's father, Dou Xun (竇勳), committed a crime and Han Yu (韓紆) tried the case. Dou Xun was arrested and executed, so when Dou Xian had gained the power, he saw an opportunity to take revenge. Han Yu was already dead at the time, but Dou sent his assassinators to kill Han's son. He cut Han's head and brought it to his father's grave, but nobody dared to object him.

Dou Xian became so powerful that even Emperor He could not get in contact with him. However, he had a faithful eunuch called Zheng Zhong (鄭眾), and they decided to kill Dou Xian, although Emperor He thought it was not morally right to kill his uncle. He even checked historical records to see if there was any Emperor who had done something similar before. Later, Emperor He deployed troops against Dou Xian and killed his loyal subjects, but he would not officially execute Dou Xian, so he exiled him and forced him to commit suicide. Emperor He gained back what was rightfully his, and his rule was generally a good one after Emperor Ming and Zhao. However, he died of disease when he was 27 years old.

Emperor's He newborn son, Liu Long (劉隆), who was less than a year old, became his successor. He was Emperor Shang of Han (漢殤帝). He was not Emperor He's first born son, but most of his older brothers were dead when they were young. Emperor He suspected that the nobility and eunuchs killed his sons, so he sent his remaining princes out of the palace. Empress Hexi (和熹皇后) became the one who took care of the royal court. She was not another Empress Dou only at this time; her policy generally helped maintain the prosperity of the Han kingdom. Unfortunately, Emperor Shang died at 1 year of age just, 220 days after he ascended to the throne. He was the youngest among all Emperors throughout Chinese history.

After Emperor Shang died, Empress Hexi became the grand empress dowager. She and her brother, Deng Zhi (鄧騭), installed 13-year-old Liu Hu (劉祜) as the next Emperor. He was the grandson of Emperor Zhang and was known as Emperor An (漢安帝). Still, the grand empress and her brother held most of the power and made all the decisions. Their allies include the eunuch Zheng Zhong and an officer called Cai Lun (蔡倫), who was famous for inventing paper. Dissatisfied by having the royal court controlled by these people, other officers planned to kill them and even Emperor An, so that they could install Liu Sheng (劉勝) as their Emperor. The grand empress heard of the rebellion and sent her army to attack them before they did. When Emperor An was 26 years old, an officer Du Gen (杜根) proposed to the grand empress that she should transfer back her power to the Emperor. Angered by Du's suggestion, she killed him with baton and deposed his corpse out of the city.

After grand empress Deng died, Emperor An took matters into his own hands. However, a group of eunuchs had already gained excessive power in the palace. The Dou family planned a revolt but failed. Deng Zhi died soon after. Without the Dou family, the eunuchs had less competitors. Emperor An even made two eunuchs Jiang Jing (江京) and Li Guo (李國) as marquis. His wet nurse, Wang Sheng (王聖), and her daughter, (伯榮) interfered with political affairs, but the Emperor did not stop them. A loyal officer, Yang Zhen, (楊震) urged the king to reduce their power, but the Emperor didn't listen. The eunuchs then framed him for siding with Deng Zhi. Yang hated himself for being so powerless that he could not kill those malicious people but was instead framed by them. He drank poison and committed suicide.

Besides the Deng family and the eunuchs, Emperor An's spouse, Empress Yan (閻皇后) was also power-hungry. She was the Emperor's favorite, but she bore no child. Left with only a few options, the Emperor made Liu Bao (劉保), who born to Consort Li (李氏), as the Crown Prince. Consort Li was already dead at the time; she was poisoned by Empress Yan. The empress feared the Crown Prince might take revenge on her after he became the next Emperor. She allied herself to the eunuch, Fan Feng (樊豐), to frame and execute the Crown Prince's wet nurse, Wang Nan (王男), and other people who were loyal to Liu Bao. She then persuaded the Emperor to depose the Crown Prince. The Emperor listened to his woman and made Liu Bao a marquis instead.

A few years later, the Xiongnu attacked and entered the Four States of Hexi (河西四郡). Many officers suggested to give up the land and retreat the army, but Zhang Dang (張當) and Chen Zhong (陳忠) insisted otherwise. Meanwhile, a lot of foreign countries were dissatisfied by Ren Shang (任尚), a diplomat after the famous Ban Chao. The Emperor then sent Ban Chao's son Ban Yong (班勇) to settle both issues and resume the good relationship between the Han empire and other countries. There was also a eleven-year-long battle with the Qiang people (羌族), which speedily emptied the national monetary reserve.

In 125, Emperor An and empress Yan travelled to the south together. The Emperor died of disease on his way back to the palace. Overall, a lot of issues arose during the time of Emperor An, especially the contention between nobility and eunuchs, as well as the weakening empire against foreign powers.

After Emperor An died, grand empress dowager Yan and her brother, Yan Xian (閻顯), installed a young prince, Liu Yi (劉懿), as the Emperor, but the Yan family was in fact in charge of the political affairs and royal duties. He was Emperor Qianshao (東漢前少帝), but some scholars do not regard him as an official Emperor. He reigned for approximately seven months before he died of disease. The eunuch Sun Cheng (孫程) used the opportunity to kill Yan Xian and Jiang Jing (a eunuch on the empress's side); they installed Liu Bao, the deposed Crown

Prince, as the next Emperor. He was known as Emperor Shun (漢順帝).

Emperor Shun cleared the Yan family and moved the grand empress out of the palace. He made the eunuchs who got him back his throne marquis. The Emperor trusted the eunuchs and transferred greater political power to them. Meanwhile, his spouse, empress Liang (梁皇后), gained enormous power for her family as well. The Liang family colluded with the eunuchs in the royal court; the corrupted government made the Han kingdom even worse. Emperor Shun died after 19 years of reign, passing his throne to his son Liu Bing (劉炳), who was known as Emperor Chong (漢沖帝).

Emperor Chong was only a year old when he ascended to the throne. He was born Consort Yu (虞貴人), but Empress Liang, who already had excessive power in the royal court, became a grand empress dowager to take care of all the political affairs. Emperor Chong died shortly after a year. The grand empress and her brother, Liang Ji (梁冀), thus installed the great-grandson of Emperor Zhang, Liu Zuan (劉纘). He was Emperor Zhi (漢質帝).

Emperor Zhi was only 8 years old at the time. The Liang family therefore continued to make the major decisions for the king. Liang Ji was so arrogant that most officers publicly criticized him, but they were effortlessly oppressed by Liang. Although Emperor Zhi was an innocent child, he noticed that Liang was far more superior than any of his officer. Once, he called Liang "an arrogant general" in the royal court. Angered by the Emperor's 'insult', he decided that Liu Zuan would not be easily controlled especially after he grew up, so he poisoned the Emperor and killed the then nine-year-old child. Liang Ji installed Liu Zhi (劉志) as the new Emperor.

The End of the Han Dynasty

The new Emperor Liu Zhi was known as Emperor Huan (漢桓帝). He had a luxurious life but did not fulfill many of his duties as an Emperor. His rule marked the downfall of the Han kingdom. For the first 13 years of his reign, he was generally considered a puppet monarch controlled by grand empress Liang. He was never the true leader of the kingdom until the last 8 years. Emperor Huan pretended to show reverence for Liang Ji, but once his empress, who was the younger sister of Liang, died, he allied himself to five eunuchs, Tang Heng (唐衡), Dan Chao (單超), Zuo Guan (左倌), Xu Huang (徐璜) and Ju Yuan (具瑗), and planned a conspiracy against the Liang family. They had a thousand of people surrounded Liang's mansion. Liang committed suicide then, but many celebrated his death.

Emperor Huan then made the five eunuchs marquis, but the powerful marquis were worse than Liang Ji. The Emperor realized the issue, so he later transferred their power to other eunuchs. He imposed heavy punishments on them for their crimes and misbehaviors as well. The Zuo brothers committed suicide and Ju Yuan was dismissed. Although the Emperor had suppressed their power to consolidate his, it was simply not enough. The marquis and other eunuchs were still harsh on the people, and corrupted. One would expect a revolt against the corrupted government, and it did happen with the students criticizing the eunuchs publicly in the city. Li Ying (李膺) was the leader; he was respected by many for his courage against the eunuchs. The eunuchs thus framed him for grouping with the students to subvert the central power. More than 200 people, including Li Ying, were arrested and none of them were allowed to become officials in their lifetime.

Emperor Huan had lots of spouses; he even had three empresses in succession, including empress Liang, empress Deng (鄧皇后), and empress Dou (竇皇后). The Emperor actually loved a consort named Tian Sheng (田聖) and wanted to make her empress, but many objected because Tian came from a low-status family. Empress Dou became envious of Tian, and so after Emperor Huan died, she first killed Tian and swore to kill all other consorts as well. Fortunately, she changed her mind after many persuaded her not to. Empress Dou and her father, Dou Wu (竇武), became the decision-makers in the royal court. They installed Liu Hong (劉宏) as next Emperor, because Emperor Huan did not have a son, in spite of a rich sex life with hundreds of women. The new Emperor was known as Emperor Ling of Han (漢靈帝).

To show his gratitude for Dou's support, young Emperor Ling made many from the Dou family dukes and marquis, making them even more powerful. Dou Wu then secretly collaborated with an official, Chen Fan (陳藩), to get rid of the powerful eunuchs. However, their plan was discovered by the eunuchs including Wang Fu (王甫) and Cao Jie (曹節). The Dou and Chen clans were wiped out, only a few were exiled. Wang later framed the Emperor's uncle, Liu Kui (劉悝), for rebellion and got him arrested as well. Liu committed suicide in prison. He also framed empress Song (宋皇后) for practising witchcraft against the king; she was deposed and later died of depression. Meanwhile, the generals, such as Lu Zhi (盧植), settled most of the border conflicts.

Emperor Ling became very positive about prospects for the country. He trusted his officers and eunuchs to take good care of the royal court, and so he focused more on having a luxurious life than improving the condition of his country. Similar to what Emperor Huan did, he ordered to have most of the scholars arrested after taking the advice from Cao Jie. Angered by the rule of the Liu government, a Taoist religious leader, Zhang Jue (張角), started a peasant revolt called the Yellow Turban Rebellion (黃巾起義). Left with no options, Emperor Ling released the scholars and sent his army against the revolts. At this point, many suffered from the social upheaval and despised the government. Soon, Emperor Ling died and his son Liu Bian (劉辯) ascended to the throne. He was known as Emperor Shao (漢少帝) or simply Prince of Hongnong (弘農王) because his reign didn't even last for a year. A general named Dong Zhuo (董卓) deposed him and installed Liu Xie (劉協) instead as his puppet monarch; the new Emperor was known as Emperor Xian (漢獻帝). Besides Dong Zhuo, Cao Cao (曹操) the Chancellor, also had enormous power.

Feeling bitter about being inferior to Cao, Emperor Xian planned to kill him but failed. His spouse, empress Fu (伏皇后), urged her father to kill Cao as well, but the conspiracy was discovered and Cao Cao denounced the empress. When empress Fu cried for her husband, Emperor Xian merely answered sadly, "I do not even know when my life would end." His two sons who were born to empress Fu were both poisoned, and the Fu family was nearly wiped out. The Han kingdom were gradually divided into three portions, starting a period known as the Three Kingdoms (三國).

Online Resources

Other books about Chinese history by Charles River Editors

Other books about the Han Dynasty on Amazon

Bibliography

Adshead, Samuel Adrian Miles (2000), China in World History, London: MacMillan Press, ISBN 0-312-22565-2.

Akira, Hirakawa (1998), A History of Indian Buddhism: From Sakyamani to Early Mahayana, translated by Paul Groner, New Delhi: Jainendra Prakash Jain At Shri Jainendra Press, ISBN 81-208-0955-6.

An, Jiayao (2002), "When glass was treasured in China", in Juliano, Annette L.; Lerner, Judith A., Silk Road Studies VII: Nomads, Traders, and Holy Men Along China's Silk Road, Turnhout: Brepols Publishers, pp. 79–94, ISBN 2-503-52178-9.

Bailey, H.W. (1985), Indo-Scythian Studies being Khotanese Texts Volume VII, Cambridge University Press, ISBN 978-0-521-11992-4.

Balchin, Jon (2003), Science: 100 Scientists Who Changed the World, New York: Enchanted Lion Books, ISBN 1-59270-017-9.

Ball, Warwick (2016), Rome in the East: Transformation of an Empire, London & New York: Routledge, ISBN 978-0-415-72078-6.

Barbieri-Low, Anthony J. (2007), Artisans in Early Imperial China, Seattle & London: University of Washington Press, ISBN 0-295-98713-8.

Barnes, Ian (2007), Mapping History: World History, London: Cartographica, ISBN 978-1-84573-323-0.

Beck, Mansvelt (1986), "The fall of Han", in Twitchett, Denis; Loewe, Michael, The Cambridge History of China: Volume I: the Ch'in and Han Empires, 221 B.C. – A.D. 220, Cambridge: Cambridge University Press, pp. 317–376, ISBN 978-0-521-24327-8.

Berggren, Lennart; Borwein, Jonathan M.; Borwein, Peter B. (2004), Pi: A Source Book, New York: Springer, ISBN 0-387-20571-3.

Bielenstein, Hans (1980), The Bureaucracy of Han Times, Cambridge: Cambridge University Press, ISBN 0-521-22510-8.

——— (1986), "Wang Mang, the Restoration of the Han Dynasty, and Later Han", in Twitchett, Denis; Loewe, Michael, The Cambridge History of China: Volume I: the Ch'in and Han Empires, 221 B.C. – A.D. 220, Cambridge: Cambridge University Press, pp. 223–290, ISBN 978-0-521-24327-8.

Block, Leo (2003), To Harness the Wind: A Short History of the Development of Sails, Annapolis: Naval Institute Press, ISBN 1-55750-209-9.

Bower, Virginia (2005), "Standing man and woman", in Richard, Naomi Noble, Recarving China's Past: Art, Archaeology and Architecture of the 'Wu Family Shrines', New Haven and London: Yale University Press and Princeton University Art Museum, pp. 242–245, ISBN 0-300-10797-8.

Bowman, John S. (2000), Columbia Chronologies of Asian History and Culture, New York: Columbia University Press, ISBN 0-231-11004-9.

Buisseret, David (1998), Envisioning the City: Six Studies in Urban Cartography, Chicago: University Of Chicago Press, ISBN 0-226-07993-7.

Bulling, A. (1962), "A landscape representation of the Western Han period", Artibus Asiae, 25 (4): 293–317, JSTOR 3249129.

Chang, Chun-shu (2007), The Rise of the Chinese Empire: Volume II; Frontier, Immigration, & Empire in Han China, 130 B.C. – A.D. 157, Ann Arbor: University of Michigan Press, ISBN 0-472-11534-0.

Chavannes, Édouard (1907), "Les pays d'Occident d'après le Heou Han chou" (PDF), T'oung pao, 8: 149–244.

Ch'en, Ch'i-Yün (1986), "Confucian, Legalist, and Taoist thought in Later Han", in Twitchett, Denis; Loewe, Michael, Cambridge History of China: Volume I: the Ch'in and Han Empires, 221 B.C. – A.D. 220, Cambridge: Cambridge University Press, pp. 766–806, ISBN 978-0-521-24327-8.

Ch'ü, T'ung-tsu (1972), Dull, Jack L., ed., Han Dynasty China: Volume 1: Han Social Structure, Seattle and London: University of Washington Press, ISBN 0-295-95068-4.

Chung, Chee Kit (2005), "Longyamen is Singapore: The Final Proof?", Admiral Zheng He & Southeast Asia, Singapore: Institute of Southeast Asian Studies, ISBN 981-230-329-4.

Cotterell, Maurice (2004), The Terracotta Warriors: The Secret Codes of the Emperor's Army, Rochester: Bear and Company, ISBN 1-59143-033-X.

Cribb, Joe (1978), "Chinese lead ingots with barbarous Greek inscriptions", Coin Hoards, London, 4: 76–78.

Csikszentmihalyi, Mark (2006), Readings in Han Chinese Thought, Indianapolis and Cambridge: Hackett Publishing Company, ISBN 0-87220-710-2.

Cullen, Christoper (2006), Astronomy and Mathematics in Ancient China: The Zhou Bi Suan Jing, Cambridge: Cambridge University Press, ISBN 0-521-03537-6.

Cutter, Robert Joe (1989), The Brush and the Spur: Chinese Culture and the Cockfight, Hong Kong: The Chinese University of Hong Kong, ISBN 962-201-417-8.

Dauben, Joseph W. (2007), "Chinese Mathematics", in Katz, Victor J., The Mathematics of Egypt, Mesopotamia, China, India, and Islam: A Sourcebook, Princeton: Princeton University Press, pp. 187–384, ISBN 0-691-11485-4.

Davis, Paul K. (2001), 100 Decisive Battles: From Ancient Times to the Present, New York: Oxford University Press, ISBN 0-19-514366-3.

Day, Lance; McNeil, Ian (1996), Biographical Dictionary of the History of Technology, New York: Routledge, ISBN 0-415-06042-7.

de Crespigny, Rafe (2007), A Biographical Dictionary of Later Han to the Three Kingdoms (23–220 AD), Leiden: Koninklijke Brill, ISBN 90-04-15605-4.

Demiéville, Paul (1986), "Philosophy and religion from Han to Sui", in Twitchett, Denis; Loewe, Michael, Cambridge History of China: Volume I: the Ch'in and Han Empires, 221 B.C. – A.D. 220, Cambridge: Cambridge University Press, pp. 808–872, ISBN 978-0-521-24327-8.

Deng, Yingke (2005), Ancient Chinese Inventions, translated by Wang Pingxing, Beijing: China Intercontinental Press (五洲传播出版社), ISBN 7-5085-0837-8.

Di Cosmo, Nicola (2002), Ancient China and Its Enemies: The Rise of Nomadic Power in East Asian History, Cambridge: Cambridge University Press, ISBN 0-521-77064-5.

Ebrey, Patricia Buckley (1974), "Estate and family management in the Later Han as seen in the Monthly Instructions for the Four Classes of People", Journal of the Economic and Social History of the Orient, 17 (2): 173–205, JSTOR 3596331.

———— (1986), "The Economic and Social History of Later Han", in Twitchett, Denis; Loewe, Michael, Cambridge History of China: Volume I: the Ch'in and Han Empires, 221 B.C. – A.D. 220, Cambridge: Cambridge University Press, pp. 608–648, ISBN 978-0-521-24327-8.

———— (1999), The Cambridge Illustrated History of China, Cambridge: Cambridge University Press, ISBN 0-521-66991-X.

Fairbank, John K.; Goldman, Merle (1998), China: A New History, Enlarged Edition, Cambridge: Harvard University Press, ISBN 0-674-11673-9.

Fraser, Ian W. (2014), "Zhang Heng 张衡", in Brown, Kerry, The Berkshire Dictionary of Chinese Biography, Great Barrington: Berkshire Publishing, ISBN 1-933782-66-8.

Greenberger, Robert (2006), The Technology of Ancient China, New York: Rosen Publishing Group, ISBN 1-4042-0558-6.

Guo, Qinghua (2005), Chinese Architecture and Planning: Ideas, Methods, and Techniques, Stuttgart and London: Edition Axel Menges, ISBN 3-932565-54-1.

Hansen, Valerie (2000), The Open Empire: A History of China to 1600, New York & London: W.W. Norton & Company, ISBN 0-393-97374-3.

Hardy, Grant (1999), Worlds of Bronze and Bamboo: Sima Qian's Conquest of History, New York: Columbia University Press, ISBN 0-231-11304-8.

Hill, John E. (2009), Through the Jade Gate to Rome: A Study of the Silk Routes during the Later Han Dynasty, 1st to 2nd Centuries AD, Charleston, South Carolina: BookSurge, ISBN 978-1-4392-2134-1.

Hinsch, Bret (2002), Women in Imperial China, Lanham: Rowman & Littlefield Publishers, ISBN 0-7425-1872-8.

Hsu, Cho-Yun (1965), "The changing relationship between local society and the central political power in Former Han: 206 B.C. – 8 A.D.", Comparative Studies in Society and History, 7 (4): 358–370, doi:10.1017/S0010417500003777.

Hsu, Elisabeth (2001), "Pulse diagnostics in the Western Han: how mai and qi determine bing", in Hsu, Elisabeth, Innovations in Chinese Medicine, Cambridge, New York, Oakleigh, Madrid, and Cape Town: Cambridge University Press, pp. 51–92, ISBN 0-521-80068-4.

Hsu, Mei-ling (1993), "The Qin maps: a clue to later Chinese cartographic development", Imago Mundi, 45: 90–100, doi:10.1080/03085699308592766.

Huang, Ray (1988), China: A Macro History, Armonk & London: M.E. Sharpe, ISBN 0-87332-452-8.

Hulsewé, A.F.P. (1986), "Ch'in and Han law", in Twitchett, Denis; Loewe, Michael, The Cambridge History of China: Volume I: the Ch'in and Han Empires, 221 B.C. – A.D. 220, Cambridge: Cambridge University Press, pp. 520–544, ISBN 978-0-521-24327-8.

Jin, Guantao; Fan, Hongye; Liu, Qingfeng (1996), "Historical Changes in the Structure of Science and Technology (Part Two, a Commentary)", in Dainian, Fan; Cohen, Robert S., Chinese Studies in the History and Philosophy of Science and Technology, translated by Kathleen Dugan and Jiang Mingshan, Dordrecht: Kluwer Academic Publishers, pp. 165–184, ISBN 0-7923-3463-9.

Knechtges, David R. (2010), "From the Eastern Han through the Western Jin (AD 25–317)", in Owen, Stephen, The Cambridge History of Chinese Literature, volume 1, Cambridge University Press, pp. 116–198, ISBN 978-0-521-85558-7.

———— (2014), "Zhang Heng 張衡", in Knechtges, David R.; Chang, Taiping, Ancient and Early Medieval Chinese Literature: A Reference Guide, Part Four, Leiden: Brill, pp. 2141–55, ISBN 978-90-04-27217-0.

Kramers, Robert P. (1986), "The development of the Confucian schools", in Twitchett, Denis; Loewe, Michael, Cambridge History of China: Volume I: the Ch'in and Han Empires, 221 B.C. – A.D. 220, Cambridge: Cambridge University Press, pp. 747–756, ISBN 978-0-521-24327-8.

Lewis, Mark Edward (2007), The Early Chinese Empires: Qin and Han, Cambridge: Harvard University Press, ISBN 0-674-02477-X.

Liu, Xujie (2002), "The Qin and Han dynasties", in Steinhardt, Nancy S., Chinese Architecture, New Haven: Yale University Press, pp. 33–60, ISBN 0-300-09559-7.

Liu, Guilin; Feng, Lisheng; Jiang, Airong; Zheng, Xiaohui (2003), "The Development of E-Mathematics Resources at Tsinghua University Library (THUL)", in Bai, Fengshan; Wegner, Bern, Electronic Information and Communication in Mathematics, Berlin, Heidelberg and New York: Springer Verlag, pp. 1–13, ISBN 3-540-40689-1.

Lloyd, Geoffrey Ernest Richard (1996), Adversaries and Authorities: Investigations into Ancient Greek and Chinese Science, Cambridge: Cambridge University Press, ISBN 0-521-55695-3.

Lo, Vivienne (2001), "The influence of nurturing life culture on the development of Western Han acumoxa therapy", in Hsu, Elisabeth, Innovation in Chinese Medicine, Cambridge, New York, Oakleigh, Madrid and Cape Town: Cambridge University Press, pp. 19–50, ISBN 0-521-80068-4.

Loewe, Michael (1968), Everyday Life in Early Imperial China during the Han Period 202 BC–AD 220, London: B.T. Batsford, ISBN 0-87220-758-7.

———— (1986), "The Former Han Dynasty", in Twitchett, Denis; Loewe, Michael, The Cambridge History of China: Volume I: the Ch'in and Han Empires, 221 B.C. – A.D. 220, Cambridge: Cambridge University Press, pp. 103–222, ISBN 978-0-521-24327-8.

———— (1994), Divination, Mythology and Monarchy in Han China, Cambridge, New York and Melbourne: Cambridge University Press, ISBN 0-521-45466-2.

———— (2005), "Funerary Practice in Han Times", in Richard, Naomi Noble, Recarving China's Past: Art, Archaeology, and Architecture of the 'Wu Family Shrines', New Haven and London: Yale University Press and Princeton University Art Museum, pp. 23–74, ISBN 0-300-10797-8.

———— (2006), The Government of the Qin and Han Empires: 221 BCE–220 CE, Hackett Publishing Company, ISBN 978-0-87220-819-3.

Mawer, Granville Allen (2013), "The Riddle of Cattigara", in Robert Nichols and Martin Woods, Mapping Our World: Terra Incognita to Australia, Canberra: National Library of Australia, pp. 38–39, ISBN 978-0-642-27809-8.

McClain, Ernest G.; Ming, Shui Hung (1979), "Chinese cyclic tunings in late antiquity", Ethnomusicology, 23 (2): 205–224, JSTOR 851462.

Morton, William Scott; Lewis, Charlton M. (2005), China: Its History and Culture (Fourth ed.), New York City: McGraw-Hill, ISBN 0-07-141279-4.

Needham, Joseph (1972), Science and Civilization in China: Volume 1, Introductory Orientations, London: Syndics of the Cambridge University Press, ISBN 0-521-05799-X.

———— (1986a), Science and Civilization in China: Volume 3; Mathematics and the Sciences of the Heavens and the Earth, Taipei: Caves Books, ISBN 0-521-05801-5.

———— (1986b), Science and Civilization in China: Volume 4, Physics and Physical Technology; Part 1, Physics, Taipei: Caves Books, ISBN 0-521-05802-3.

——— (1986c), Science and Civilisation in China: Volume 4, Physics and Physical Technology; Part 2, Mechanical Engineering, Taipei: Caves Books, ISBN 0-521-05803-1.

——— (1986d), Science and Civilization in China: Volume 4, Physics and Physical Technology, Part 3, Civil Engineering and Nautics, Taipei: Caves Books, ISBN 0-521-07060-0.

Needham, Joseph; Tsien, Tsuen-Hsuin (1986), Science and Civilisation in China: Volume 5, Chemistry and Chemical Technology, Part 1, Paper and Printing, Taipei: Caves Books, ISBN 0-521-08690-6.

Needham, Joseph (1988), Science and Civilization in China: Volume 5, Chemistry and Chemical Technology, Part 9, Textile Technology: Spinning and Reeling, Cambridge: Cambridge University Press.

Neinhauser, William H.; Hartman, Charles; Ma, Y.W.; West, Stephen H. (1986), The Indiana Companion to Traditional Chinese Literature: Volume 1, Bloomington: Indiana University Press, ISBN 0-253-32983-3.

Nelson, Howard (1974), "Chinese maps: an exhibition at the British Library", The China Quarterly, 58: 357–362, doi:10.1017/S0305741000011346.

Nishijima, Sadao (1986), "The economic and social history of Former Han", in Twitchett, Denis; Loewe, Michael, Cambridge History of China: Volume I: the Ch'in and Han Empires, 221 B.C. – A.D. 220, Cambridge: Cambridge University Press, pp. 545–607, ISBN 978-0-521-24327-8.

Norman, Jerry (1988), Chinese, Cambridge and New York: Cambridge University Press, ISBN 0-521-29653-6.

Omura, Yoshiaki (2003), Acupuncture Medicine: Its Historical and Clinical Background, Mineola: Dover Publications, ISBN 0-486-42850-8.

O'Reilly, Dougald J.W. (2007), Early Civilizations of Southeast Asia, Lanham, New York, Toronto, Plymouth: AltaMira Press, Division of Rowman and Littlefield Publishers, ISBN 0-7591-0279-1.

Paludan, Ann (1998), Chronicle of the Chinese Emperors: the Reign-by-Reign Record of the Rulers of Imperial China, London: Thames & Hudson, ISBN 0-500-05090-2.

Pigott, Vincent C. (1999), The Archaeometallurgy of the Asian Old World, Philadelphia: University of Pennsylvania Museum of Archaeology and Anthropology, ISBN 0-924171-34-0.

Ronan, Colin A (1994), The Shorter Science and Civilization in China: 4, Cambridge: Cambridge University Press, ISBN 0-521-32995-7. (an abridgement of Joseph Needham's work)

Schaefer, Richard T. (2008), Encyclopedia of Race, Ethnicity, and Society: Volume 3, Thousand Oaks: Sage Publications Inc, ISBN 1-4129-2694-7.

Shen, Kangshen; Crossley, John N.; Lun, Anthony W.C. (1999), The Nine Chapters on the Mathematical Art: Companion and Commentary, Oxford: Oxford University Press, ISBN 0-19-853936-3.

Steinhardt, Nancy Shatzman (2004), "The Tang architectural icon and the politics of Chinese architectural history", The Art Bulletin, 86 (2): 228–254, doi:10.1080/00043079.2004.10786192, JSTOR 3177416.

————— (2005a), "Pleasure tower model", in Richard, Naomi Noble, Recarving China's Past: Art, Archaeology, and Architecture of the 'Wu Family Shrines', New Haven and London: Yale University Press and Princeton University Art Museum, pp. 275–281, ISBN 0-300-10797-8.

————— (2005b), "Tower model", in Richard, Naomi Noble, Recarving China's Past: Art, Archaeology, and Architecture of the 'Wu Family Shrines', New Haven and London: Yale University Press and Princeton University Art Museum, pp. 283–285, ISBN 0-300-10797-8.

Straffin, Philip D., Jr (1998), "Liu Hui and the first Golden Age of Chinese mathematics", Mathematics Magazine, 71 (3): 163–181, JSTOR 2691200.

Suárez, Thomas (1999), Early Mapping of Southeast Asia, Singapore: Periplus Editions, ISBN 962-593-470-7.

Sun, Xiaochun; Kistemaker, Jacob (1997), The Chinese Sky During the Han: Constellating Stars and Society, Leiden, New York, Köln: Koninklijke Brill, ISBN 90-04-10737-1.

Taagepera, Rein (1979), "Size and Duration of Empires: Growth-Decline Curves, 600 B.C. to 600 A.D.", Social Science History, 3 (3/4): 115–138, JSTOR 1170959.

Teresi, Dick (2002), Lost Discoveries: The Ancient Roots of Modern Science–from the Babylonians to the Mayas, New York: Simon and Schuster, ISBN 0-684-83718-8.

Thorp, Robert L. (1986), "Architectural principles in early Imperial China: structural problems and their solution", The Art Bulletin, 68 (3): 360–378, JSTOR 3050972.

Tom, K.S. (1989), Echoes from Old China: Life, Legends, and Lore of the Middle Kingdom, Honolulu: The Hawaii Chinese History Center of the University of Hawaii Press, ISBN 0-8248-1285-9.

Torday, Laszlo (1997), Mounted Archers: The Beginnings of Central Asian History, Durham: The Durham Academic Press, ISBN 1-900838-03-6.

Turnbull, Stephen R. (2002), Fighting Ships of the Far East: China and Southeast Asia 202 BC–AD 1419, Oxford: Osprey Publishing, ISBN 1-84176-386-1.

Wagner, Donald B. (1993), Iron and Steel in Ancient China, Brill, ISBN 978-90-04-09632-5.

——— (2001), The State and the Iron Industry in Han China, Copenhagen: Nordic Institute of Asian Studies Publishing, ISBN 87-87062-83-6.

Wang, Yu-ch'uan (1949), "An outline of The central government of the Former Han dynasty", Harvard Journal of Asiatic Studies, 12 (1/2): 134–187, JSTOR 2718206.

Wang, Zhongshu (1982), Han Civilization, translated by K.C. Chang and Collaborators, New Haven and London: Yale University Press, ISBN 0-300-02723-0.

Wang, Xudang; Li, Zuixiong; Zhang, Lu (2010), "Condition, Conservation, and Reinforcement of the Yumen Pass and Hecang Earthen Ruins Near Dunhuang", in Neville Agnew, Conservation of Ancient Sites on the Silk Road: Proceedings of the Second International Conference on the Conservation of Grotto Sites, Mogao Grottoes, Dunhuang, People's Republic of China, June 28 – July 3, 2004, pp. 351–352 [351–357], ISBN 978-1-60606-013-1.

Watson, William (2000), The Arts of China to AD 900, New Haven: Yale University Press, ISBN 0-300-08284-3.

Wiesner-Hanks, Merry E. (2011) [2001], Gender in History: Global Perspectives (2nd ed.), Oxford: Wiley-Blackwell, ISBN 978-1-4051-8995-8

Xue, Shiqi (2003), "Chinese lexicography past and present", in Hartmann, R.R.K., Lexicography: Critical Concepts, London and New York: Routledge, pp. 158–173, ISBN 0-415-25365-9.

Young, Gary K. (2001), Rome's Eastern Trade: International Commerce and Imperial Policy, 31 BC – AD 305, London & New York: Routledge, ISBN 0-415-24219-3.

Yü, Ying-shih (1967), Trade and Expansion in Han China: A Study in the Structure of Sino-Barbarian Economic Relations, Berkeley: University of California Press.

——— (1986), "Han foreign relations", in Twitchett, Denis; Loewe, Michael, The Cambridge History of China: Volume I: the Ch'in and Han Empires, 221 B.C. – A.D. 220, Cambridge: Cambridge University Press, pp. 377–462, ISBN 978-0-521-24327-8.

Yule, Henry (1915), Henri Cordier, ed., Cathay and the Way Thither: Being a Collection of Medieval Notices of China, Vol I: Preliminary Essay on the Intercourse Between China and the Western Nations Previous to the Discovery of the Cape Route, 1, London: Hakluyt Society.

Zhang, Guangda (2002), "The role of the Sogdians as translators of Buddhist texts", in Juliano, Annette L.; Lerner, Judith A., Silk Road Studies VII: Nomads, Traders, and Holy Men Along China's Silk Road, Turnhout: Brepols Publishers, pp. 75–78, ISBN 2-503-52178-9.

Zhou, Jinghao (2003), Remaking China's Public Philosophy for the Twenty-First Century, Westport: Greenwood Publishing Group, ISBN 0-275-97882-6.

Free Books by Charles River Editors

We have brand new titles available for free most days of the week. To see which of our titles are currently free, click on this link.

Discounted Books by Charles River Editors

We have titles at a discount price of just 99 cents everyday. To see which of our titles are currently 99 cents, click on this link.

Printed in Great Britain
by Amazon